Let's ESTIMATE

A Book About Estimating and Rounding Numbers

by **David A. Adler** • illustrated by **Edward Miller**

Holiday House / New York

How old are you?

Did you answer 10, 11, or 12?

What you answered is probably not your **exact** age.

It's your **approximate** age. If today is not your birthday you should have said "**about**" 10, 11, or 12.

I'm 10.

I'm 11.

I'm 12.

Of course, when someone asks your age, it would be odd to give your **exact** age. It would be odd if you answered, "I am ten years, seven months, four days, three hours, and twelve minutes old." And your age keeps changing. Now you may be ten years, seven months, four days, three hours, and twelve minutes old. Soon you'll be ten years, seven months, four days, three hours, and thirteen minutes old. When someone asks how old you are he wants to know "**about**" how old you are or how old you were on your last birthday.

Many times an approximate answer is just as good as an exact answer. Sometimes it's even better.

I am 68,000,000 years, seven months, four days, three hours, and eleven minutes old.

How old are you?

If someone were to ask you the population of the United States you might answer, "Three hundred and twenty million." For most purposes, that's a perfectly acceptable answer. But it's not an exact answer. It's an **estimation**. The population of the United States is "**about**" three hundred and twenty million.

It would be difficult to give the exact population of the United States. Each day people are born and people die. People move to the United States and people leave. The population keeps changing.

It's often important to estimate.

320 000 000 0 01 5 4 7

New York

Go back 5 spaces

Go back 2 spaces

Move 9 spaces to France

D.C.

London

Move to the U.S.

France

GO

Skip a turn

When you're food shopping it's good to estimate the total cost of all the items in your cart. You need to know you have enough money to pay for it all.

How would you estimate the total cost of the items in your cart? You might try **rounding** the cost of each item and then adding them.

When you **estimate**, you make an educated guess at an actual number.

When you **round** a number, you change it so it's easier to work with the number.

Estimating is **not** rounding. Rounding is **not** estimating. But rounding can help you to estimate.

For example, you might have a box of cereal in your cart and its cost might be $3.95. That's about four dollars, so you **round** the cost of the cereal to four dollars.

You might have a quart of milk in your cart and its cost might be $1.95. That's about two dollars, so you **round** the cost of the quart of milk to two dollars.

You might have three bananas in your cart and the cost of each might be 30¢. Together the three bananas cost about 90¢. You might even **round** the 90¢ to one dollar.

After rounding the cost of the cereal, milk, and bananas you **add** them: $4 + $2 +$1 = $7.00.

You would **estimate** the cost of the items in your cart to be $7.00.

The actual cost of the items in your cart is $6.77.

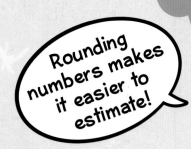

Rounding numbers makes it easier to estimate!

$3.95 rounds to $4.00

$1.95 rounds to $2.00

.90 rounds to $1.00

actual cost $6.77

$7.00
estimated cost

It's especially important to estimate when you use a calculator.

Here's a multiplication problem Sarah has for homework: **19 X 11**

19 is just 1 less than 20.

11 is just 1 more than 10.

1 2 3 4 5 6

12 13 14 15

$$20 \times 10 = 200$$

Since 20 X 10 = 200, Sarah estimates that 19 X 11 is about 200. But the answer on her calculator is 2109. That's a lot more than her estimate. She does the problem again. This time the answer on her calculator is 209.

209 is close to her estimate of 200.

$$19 \times 11 = \cancel{2109} \qquad 19 \times 11 = 209 \checkmark$$

What happened? The first time Sarah did the problem on her calculator, by mistake she multiplied 19 by 111 instead of 11. By estimating before she did the problem she knew her first answer was wrong.

If your estimate is very different from the answer on your calculator, you made a mistake.

To make her estimate, Sarah "rounded" both 19 and 11 to the nearest 10. **Rounding** is helpful when you estimate.

When you **estimate**, you guess what the actual number is.

When you **round** a number, you know the actual number but you change it to a number that is easier to use.

There are no real rules for estimating, just that you try to get close to the actual number.

There are rules for rounding. Rounding is often done to the nearest 10, the nearest 100, the nearest 1,000, and higher. When you round to the nearest 10 you look at the digit just to the right of the tens place.

If it is 5 or more you round up.

thousands	hundreds	tens	ones
		1	9

round up = 20

If it is less than 5 you round down.

thousands	hundreds	tens	ones
		1	1

round down = 10

round **up**

10
9
8
7
6
5
4
3
2
1
0

round **down**

In the number **463**

the digit 6 is in the tens place.

The digit just to its right is 3.

3 is less than 5 so you round down.

463 rounded to the nearest 10 is **460**.

thousands	hundreds	tens	ones
	4	6	3

T-Rex ate about 460 cookies.

COOKIES

round down 0 1 2 3 4 5 6 7 8 9 10 round up

In the number **1,248**,
the digit 4 is in the tens place.
The digit just to its right is 8.
8 is more than 5 so you round up.
1,248 rounded to the nearest 10 is **1,250**.

thousands	hundreds	tens	ones
1,	2	4	8

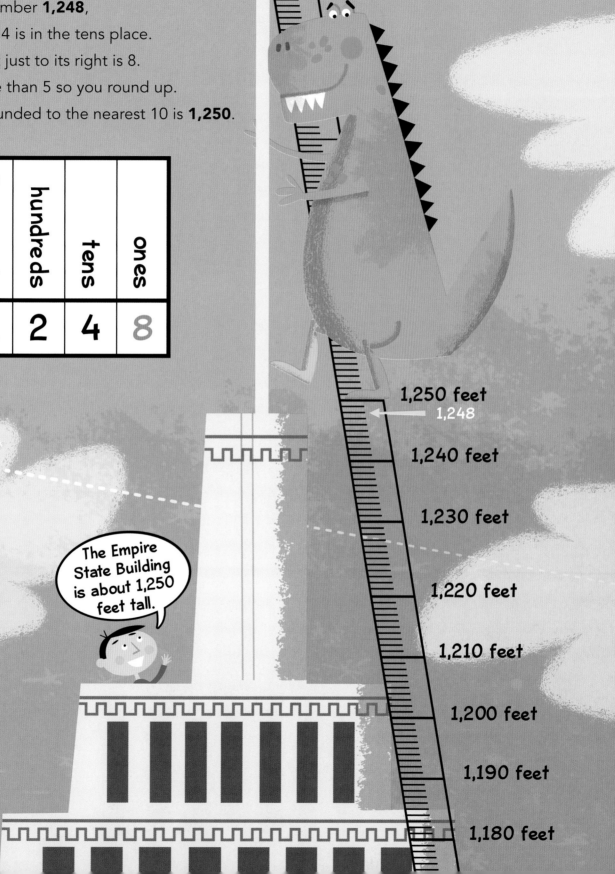

1,250 feet
1,248

1,240 feet

1,230 feet

1,220 feet

1,210 feet

1,200 feet

1,190 feet

1,180 feet

The Empire State Building is about 1,250 feet tall.

To round to the nearest 100,

look at the digit in the 100th place.

In the number **427**,

the digit 4 is in the 100th place.

The digit just to its right is 2.

2 is less than 5 so you round down.

427 rounded to the nearest 100th is **400**.

thousands	hundreds	tens	ones
	4	2	7

Dino weighs about 400 pounds.

DINO

In the number **4,162**,
the digit 1 is in
the hundredth place.
The digit just to its right is 6.
6 is more than 5 so you round up.
4,162 rounded to the nearest 100th is **4,200**.

When you round a number to the nearest 100,
all digits to the right of the 100th place
will be zeros.

thousands	hundreds	tens	ones
4,	1	6	2

To round to the nearest 1,000,

look at the digit in the 1,000th place.

In the number **2,862**,

the digit 2 is in the 1,000th place.

The digit just to its right is 8.

8 is more than 5 so you round up.

2,862 rounded to the nearest 1,000th is **3,000**.

thousands	hundreds	tens	ones
2,	8	6	2

California

START

1,000 miles

YIELD

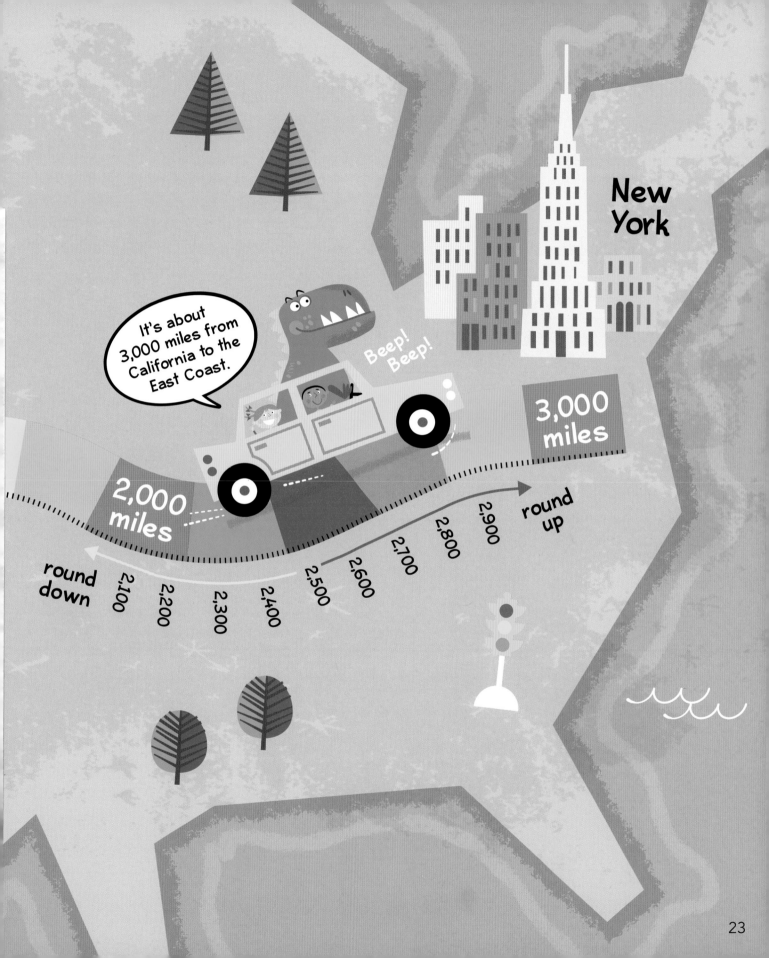

23

In the number **238,915** the digit 8 is in the 1,000th place.

The digit just to its right is 9.

9 is more than 5 so you round up.

238,915 rounded to the nearest 1,000th is **239,000**.

When you round a number to the nearest 1,000th,

all digits to the right of the 1,000th place will be zeros.

237,000 miles

236,000 miles

235,000 miles

234,000 miles

233,000 miles

232,000 miles

231,000 miles

230,000 miles

100 thousands	10 thousands	thousands	hundreds	tens	ones
2	3	8,	9	1	5

People often use rounded numbers.

When the newspaper reports that **115,000,000** (115 million) people watched the Superbowl, surely the number of viewers has been rounded to the nearest million.

People often estimate.

When you decide how much pizza to buy for a party, you are estimating how much your friends will eat.

When someone says, "I'll be at your house in 20 minutes," that's an estimate.

When someone says, "I spent $300 shopping," surely he rounded the amount he spent to the nearest $10.

Pick any two two-digit numbers. Estimate what your answer would be if you multiplied them. Use what you learned about rounding numbers to help you make your estimate. Use a calculator to multiply the numbers. How close was your estimate to the actual answer?

Estimating and rounding are very useful skills.

The more you estimate and round numbers, the better you'll get at it.

thousands	hundreds	tens	ones
		2	7

round up = 30

thousands	hundreds	tens	ones
		1	1

round down = 10

30 x 10 = 300 est.

27 x 11 = 297

How many steps does it take to walk from your house to the next? How many houses are there on your block?

Estimate how many steps it will take you to walk from one end of your block to the other. Then count as you walk.

How close was your estimate to the actual number of steps?

For Leah and Eitan
— D. A. A.

To my great-nephew, Jayden
— E. M.

Library of Congress Cataloging-in-Publication Data

Names: Adler, David A., author. | Miller, Edward, 1964– illustrator.
Title: Let's estimate : a book about estimating and rounding numbers /
by David A. Adler ; illustrated by Edward Miller.
Description: First edition | New York : Holiday House, [2017] | Audience:
Ages 6–10. | Audience: Grades 4 to 6.
Identifiers: LCCN 2016027033 | ISBN 9780823436682 (hardcover)
Subjects: LCSH: Mathematics—Juvenile literature. | Estimation theory—Juvenile literature.
| Rounding (Numerical analysis)—Juvenile literature.
Classification: LCC QA63 .A3219 2017 | DDC 513—dc23
LC record available at https://lccn.loc.gov/2016027033

Visit www.davidaadler.com for more information on the author, a list of his books, and
downloadable teacher's guides and educational materials. You can also learn more about
the writing process, take fun quizzes, and read select pages from David A. Adler's books.

Visit Edward Miller on Facebook at Edward Elementary.